FLIGHT
OF THE
WILD GOOSE

FLIGHT
OF THE
WILD GOOSE

Poetry by Janet Carncross Chandler
Photographs by Lori Burkhalter-Lackey

Papier-Mache Press

First Edition

Printed in the United States of America.

93 92 91 90 89   6 5 4 3 2 1

Some of the poems in this collection are reprinted from three volumes of poetry by Janet Carncross Chandler: *The Colors of a Marriage* (1982), *How Are You? They Ask New Widow* (1985), and *Significant Relationships* (1988). Some of the poems have appeared in *Quercus*, *City Country Miner*, *Anthology of Magazine Verse* (1980), *Io*, *Haight Ashbury Literary Review*, *Goddard Review*, NPR's Sacramento FM 91 Newsletter, and the Unitarian Universalist Society of Sacramento's Morality Exchange.

Editing: Sandra Martz
Design: Cynthia Heier
Cover art: Comstock Inc./Michael Stuckey
Typography: Pioneer Graphics

Library of Congress Cataloging-in-Publication Data

Chandler, Janet Carncross, 1910-
    Flight of the wild goose : poetry / by Janet Carncross Chandler ;   photographs by Lori Burkhalter-Lackey. — 1st ed.
        p. cm.
    ISBN 0-918949-07-6 : $8.00
    I. Title.
    PS3553.H27123F5   1989
811'.54—dc20   89-16270
                    CIP

To my sons and their families
to old and new friends
and to the many poets and teachers
who influenced my poetic growth

Contents

Chrysalis

A person who has lost a mate
is like a chrysalis
shrouded
in numbness, pain and sorrow
unaware
of the beautiful creature
growing wings within.

Leave the Top Plums

Now to pick wild plums:
first you have to look for them
and believe in serendipities
or you will never find them.

Wait until they have ripened
to a dull-gold-and-pink mellow sheen.
Plums, wild or no, are sour and good
only for spitting out if picked before they are ready.

Then on a sunny day—so the plums
will gleam and glisten through the green leaves
and show themselves to you—look up
and around, picking as you go
pulling branches down and stretching
to reach just one more plum.

It will not be easy.
Branches will prickle and stick
threaten to eliminate an eye, scratch
at your jacket—or skin if they can—
anything to protect their bounty.

Finally you have a bowlful.
Do not be greedy.   Pick only those
within your farthest reach.   Leave the top plums,
the ones high up, for birds that will
swoop down and pluck them off.

Anxiety Attack

Women's Share at Women's Center
the sign beckoned. Come next Friday.

A chance to read my poems!
So why this sniffly nose
surely a cold?
Fingers burn or cut themselves
or are run into by cactus thorns.

Part of me is scared:
I'll be the only older woman.
My throat will close
so I cannot read my poems.
My throat will not close
and I will have to read them.
None of the younger women
will like them.

Yet I am here.
To be older is good
for I have lived a while.
I have something to share.

My Old Familiar Maiden Name

I'm taking it back, my Scottish handle—
sprig of Scottish heather, prick of Scottish thistle,
the burr and the lilt of Robert Burns—
melding it in between first and last,
feeling like my old jaunty self
with my old familiar maiden name
open to the world, not tucked in my pocket.
No disrespect meant, dear William.
Yours (ours) is a good name, and I'm glad
to have it for our last name,
but not right next to my skin, next
to my good Scottish first name.

Bright Strand of Sunny Yellow

My sex is
an indelible part of me
bright strand of sunny yellow
woven through the fabric of my life:

    a cuddle on Father's lap
    (wishing Mother would disappear)
    slumber parties with five best friends
    the thrill of the Junior Prom

    our hard, lean, early years
    (nights kept us close)
    seeing you in our twin sons.

Still strong, that rhythmic tide.
I'm glad I am my female sex.

Together in the Dark

lying here
warmed by our bodies' heat
and the comfort of the many-years-married
we listen to the light touch
of rain on the roof.

Your right hand wonders if this is a night
for love, settles for a light and friendly touch.
I tuck the covers around your ear
the way you like them.

I drift off
this moment in sharp focus —
all others, clouds...trailing.

The Colors of a Marriage

Golden
that's what they call it, this,
our fiftieth year. Yet
nothing stays golden forever.

Marriage sometimes seems like a wave
two horses cresting together,
or a plane taking off or landing
with a couple of amateurs at the controls;
in a temporary lull, like
two snails creeping along, a little ridiculous
not seeming to know where they're going
but getting there, leaving
an irridescent wavy line in their wake.

The colors of a marriage are in sea or earth tones
changing as we concentrate on them
with occasional glints or flashes
and, when we least expect,
a back-lit glory
that has kept us together
since June 18, fifty years ago.

Encouraging Lines

to a young couple
about to celebrate their first anniversary
from an older couple
approaching their fiftieth

We find a kind of silkiness
between us
as we grow older   together
like wood worn from rubbing against
bumping into
turning back
starting over
vowing never
slogging behind
wondering why
opening up—
to discover our own patina,
"something grown beautiful
with age and use."

Security Blanket

How could I ever cope
with birth and death
and all the perils in between
without:

    smell of bacon crisping
    push of wind against my rake
    contented sound of corn-fed ducks
    feel of pen with poem in mind
    stroke of your voice and touch?

Resistance

We are learning to play a new word game.
It is not electronic.
It costs no money.

We speak in zigzag sentences.
Our words zoom past like buzzing insects
or meander, missing meaning.

*"One of these days, I suppose I'd better
show you how to check the air gauge on the tires."*
"After all these years of you doing it?"

"Usually, I let the bed air once a week."
"Why tell me?"

"Here! I'll show you how to start the furnace."
"Not right now, dear, I'm getting lunch."

"The trick in making angel food
is to measure the dry ingredients first
then you beat the eggs to peaks."
"Whatever way you do is fine with me."

Our new word game is a little like Sanskrit. Or Braille.
It is an older couples' game.

Seven Snaps of the Shutter

I am alone in a skiff skimming downstream.
The water roils about my tiny craft.
Impulse to take my photograph
is thwarted: the camera is at home.
Trees and shrubs rush past. I grab for them.
My hands are raw and bleeding.

Someone is watching from the bank.
A boy child, very young, curious
about where I'm going.

In a flat-bottomed rowboat, a man sits
by himself in the middle of a lake.
The water is still. He has no oars.
He knows he is not going anywhere,
rather likes the idea. His fingers
trail through warm water.

Now I am in a eucalyptus grove near the ocean.
I seem to be a long strand of bark,
shredded and finally torn from the trunk
by wind. I have given up clinging
to my ancient tree, am whipped around
in spirals and whorls by an increasingly stiff wind.

I think back to my life of attachment.
Dense fog shrouds the sensations I once knew.
I try without success to feel myself into the future.

14

A feeling of suspension, of drifting.
The wind has lessened.
I have convinced myself
I am not concerned with whether
I *could* make a stand against the air currents.

The wind is dying down.
I have been waiting for this moment for years.

Loss and Healing

When we came, China
was in bloom...now you are gone
even the trees weep.

William Smith Chandler died in Chongqing, China on October 12, 1984, while he and Janet were on a trip. This senryu was written for his cremation service in China and for a celebration of his life in Auburn, California.

16

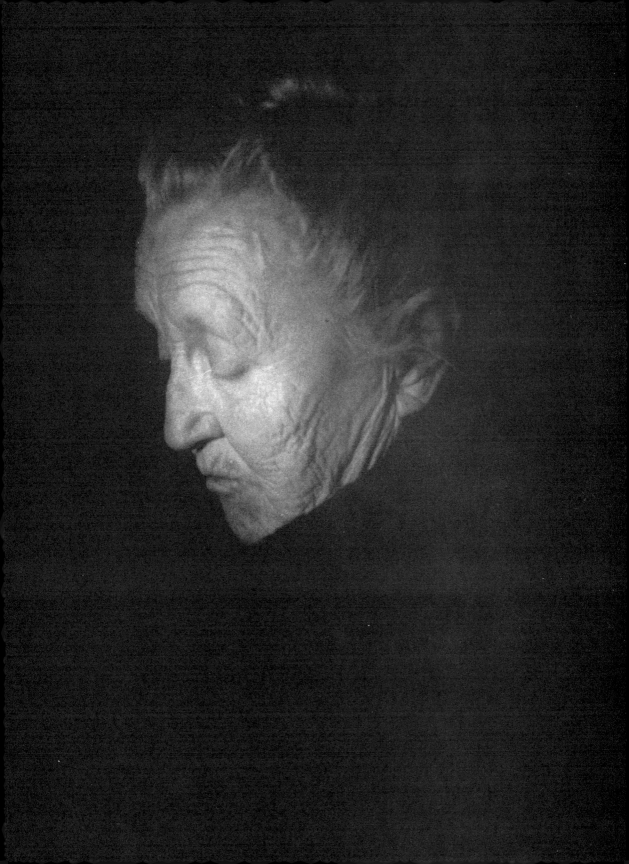

Newly Remembered

After you've consulted your lawyer,
applied at Social Security for Death Benefits
(that contradiction in terms)
sent off four Death Certificates, all originals,
to those mystics you paid
to keep evil from your door,
after you've discovered you *can* face each day
if you cried enough the night before

after you've celebrated his life
with relatives and friends,
told how he died in China and how
wonderfully cared for,
how thankful you are to be home again

after you've shared his new London Fog raincoat,
his well loved jacket with your twin sons,
given his enlarger to the sturdy neighbor
he was so sure would appear
instantaneously
and carry him out of the hospital
over the ocean, and deposit him in his own bed

after you've learned how easy
it is to cook for one (and how dull to eat alone!)
gone through his books and clothes and tools
(they tell me this can take months
and exact a toll in pain revisited)
after you've lost your new budget book three times
find you've forgotten why you made a trip to town

newly remembered bits of wisdom
may return to you, straight from him:
Make a daily list each night, so you can sleep—
and cross things off next day;
if you lose something around the house,
think of why you might *want* to lose it.

Network

People I didn't even know
knew me well enough to care
whether I laugh or cry
write notes of condolence
relating my loss implicity to theirs.
As they pile up, these notes,
and are answered, slowly
because all movement is glacial these days,
I sense I am one part
of a healing network
of humans who too
have loved and shared and given birth,
faced death and lost,
only to feel our new selves burst,
painful, yet new-green,
out of a cut brown branch
surely past all hope of greening.

"How Are You?"

They ask new widow, hoping she won't tell

If a little coral edges out New Widow Gray,
her eyes   so dull and vacant
red-rimmed each morning
take on a livelier look—

her slowed   unfocused walk
each foot waiting for the order:
FORGE FORWARD,
resembles even slightly the old
confident stride of one who knows
where going   how to get there—

her speech   halting or absent
not always quite relevant to what was asked
speaking unsureness as to whether to speak at all,
now seems more like her burbling brook
with shallows   deeps   even
an occasional laughing rill—

you'll know she is ready to begin
finding out her real identity
no longer merely husband's wife.
Or maybe she's only fooled
herself   and maybe you   pretending
she's found another and a life ahead—

creating a protective scab
to cover her deep wound
sealing it off until healing wells up from within.

Touching Base

Until tonight, no dream has been tough enough
to survive waking's barriers since you died.
Only fragments, hinting of fearsome
sights I could not face.
On my way home from Port Townsend, two dreams:

In the first, wan and insubstantial,
you stand on one side of a chasm,
arms outstretched, one foot poised
to cross over. Then you vanish.

In the second, I make my way alone down
endless steps. Below, a surging sound and darkness.
Finally, I decide I cannot continue, begin
the long climb back up. Despite
the steepness of the steps
I leap toward morning light.

Do I then still think of death, of dying?
Not consciously. Sometimes, when I come upon
a letter in your left-hand slant, inadvertently
touch your pillow flat against mine,
I think I can bear this loneliness no longer.
Then one or the other son phones.
Or I phone them. Ask a friend to dinner.
Or a new poem floats into view,
demands a hearing and a voice, and I give thanks
once more for blessed consciousness.

Trash Man

Last night, after selling
the first of Bill's hundreds of books,
having convinced myself someone might as well
be reading about the Civil War,
I found his glasses staring at me.
I had carried them home from China,
in lieu of their owner,
placed them just below his photograph, within
easy arm's reach. He made no move
to put them on, though
he could not see a word without them.
Gradually, they took on a dead appearance,
no longer part of his face, lost the patina
that graced them when he was alive,
just lay there, inert, inanimate —
until they started staring.

This morning, knowing the trash man
will come by, I cover your glasses
with your grimy garden hat,
tie both inside a plastic bag, place
it on top of a pile of trash.
Even the trees weep on this gray morning
when the trash man hoists that can
into his cavernous machine, grave
for dead things like old hats and unused glasses.

Living with a Man

is like living with the wind.
Sometimes he'll come upon you
naked in your double bed
wrap you round   go swirling
and swooshing   you in his arms
all about the house   up   up
into the sky and home again.

Or he may go quiet   stay within himself.
You will wonder where he's gone.
There he is   reading in his recliner.

Sometimes you quarrel
and you may lock him out
excommunicate him to the garden
where you can hear him growl and grumble
go sullen or roar
demanding to be let in.
"This is my house!" he'll bellow.
"*Our* house!" you remind him.

Oh, what an empty place
no man in house or garden.

I Am Learning to Live Alone

Something happened on my visit
to my far-living son-and-family.
When I got back, our home had turned—
all by itself, no help from me—
into *my* home. To think, I almost ran
away into who knows what misery.

My home can't run itself.
So now I have to decide
who's going to do what—and when.
That's easy. Only one of me.
So I'm the one to cook and clean,
pull the weeds, choose between
Sweet Lady tulips and Siberian squill.
Simple. Why not both?

Seven hours a week inside, seven out.
Sounds about right. Distributed
as I please. If I spend six
painting the trellis
the floor may get another lick and promise.
Sleeping laps up seven hours a night, naps
as close to an hour as I can spare.
Reparative time I can't afford
to stint at my age.

Let's see. Fourteen plus fifty-six
makes seventy. Subtract from one hundred sixty-eight.
Almost one hundred left—for friends and families,
poetry, photography, volunteering.
Of course I'll invite Bill back
now and again, longtime
trusted confidant and consultant.
But you know what they say about consultants.

My Love Has Gone

and no new love
has come to take his place.
No one is in sight.
Mile on distant mile
no trees or flowering shrubs
only a coyote
howling alone on moonlit nights.

Enough of howling!
My poet-friends have been patient
but there's a limit to their willingness
to listen to yet one more
poem of lament.
And, yes, a limit to my need
to write one.

Ah! The coyote pricks her ears.
An answering call?
Perhaps, if she simply waits—
only an occasional soft whine
to signal her presence—
another will come, in reality
or at least in fantasy.
And if none comes?
She will settle down to cope
with harsh joys,
arid country.

Thirty-Seven Varieties

We stop by an ice-cream store on our way home.
My new friend seems to need
me to say how I feel before he can dare
to say (or maybe even
let himself know) how he feels.
Sensing possible retreat,
I see myself reach out,
try to keep my voice tuned low,
not seem too forward, want only
to hear his voice, see his smile, his quick
sharp glance take me in.
Peppermint seems about right for me.
Maybe lemon.   My new friend, clearly
used to plain vanilla, dares more often now
to show his wild, wild cherry side.

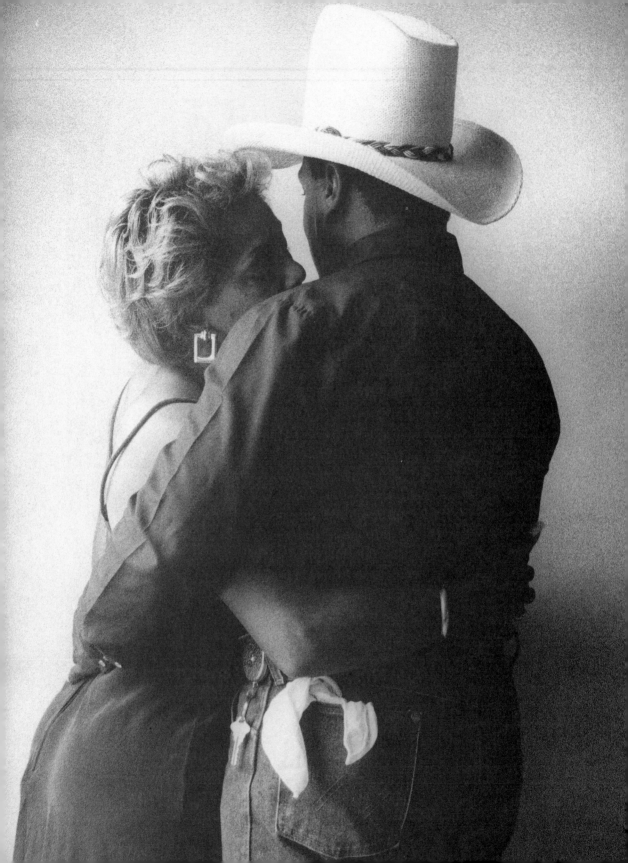

Relearning the Hug

After a bleak period

It begins with a tingle in my toes
flows swiftly upward
through my body
gently blooms in my pelvis
blurs my vision
excites my heart
extends my arms until
the whole of you and the whole of me
are wound round in one
joyful enveloping hug.

Ancient Adage

Smarting from the chastening
experience of rejection
by a man who offered me
a whitely chaste kiss
in lieu of love,
because I forgot
that men like to be
the chasers
not the chased,

I offer you, my sisters,
this valuable advice:

when you feel stirrings,
pulsings, urgings
you thought
you might never feel again,
and reach out to touch the one
who gave these gifts
by tossing a winsome smile,

you may be tempted, as I
to respond so warmly
so freely, that he,
until then thinking me
attractive, possibly someone he
might like to
invite out for dinner,

took flight, leaving behind only
that frosty kiss,
bleak reminder.

Questions

SHE

I've thought and thought,
how to phrase this so felicitously
you'll not take offense...
There's no way but openly.

So—
How did you manage about sex,
my dear, my very dear, my almost-love,
all those years I was married
to one man, raising our children?

Was there one woman...two...
a dozen...more?
Or was a man your close companion...
or several men, or even boys?

Your answer is my *sine qua non*
before I put on my Beads of Availability
as the Dinka women do when they are ready.

HE

And now I've given you *my* answer...
my turn to ask.
Was there by chance (or otherwise)
one time, only one...
or, forgive me, more...
when you briefly broke your marriage vows
with one...or several...lovers
of either sex?

What's fair for one these days
is fair for both, my dear, you
who will be, I hope, my only-love.
I'm eager to admire your beads.

Spring

Sitting close
fingers twining, untwining, intertwining
finding hills, valleys, secret places,
the part of me
I thought dead
comes bursting into life.
Spring is not due outside
for many months.   Inside, tonight
we have created our own spring
testing how best we fit each other.

What could be more sensuous
more wildly exciting
than the touch
the musky scent of you
seeking me out as I seek you,
our hearts pounding yes.

Revision

The other tenants
are getting used
to seeing me
arrive each Saturday,
my arms grasping
a brown paper bag,
seeing me ring Unauthorized Personnel Welcome
then disappear into your apartment.

I no longer worry
over what they think of me.
Either they know that two
can share dinner
and an evening
in one apartment,
and what goes on inside—
or doesn't—
is nobody else's business,
or else they don't
and who cares anyhow?

Love

is like a river.
Sometimes it flows smoothly
wide as the Mississippi
or the blood red Yangtze,
stretches out before us   a lifetime.

Yet the flow
is subject to sudden currents
push/pulled to left   to right,
unexpected boulders,
pileup of sand and debris.

We know for certain our course
will be perilous   filled with uncertainties.
Can we be sure of the strength
the power
the pull of attraction,

trust it to carry us along   help us survive
shoals   gorges   cliffs on either side
fog in early morning and evening?
Will sun pierce through
when we can see no light ahead?

Remember those first
rivulets of feeling
our fingers   then our bodies
finding each other   easing our aloneness.

We strain to see the future.
With luck and loving care
we could have years together —
If we remember:
we share a river of love.
Only *we* can keep trash from tearing us apart.

When You're in Love

suddenly
the world is made up
of mountains and valleys.

Was it only
yesterday I felt sure you planned
to leave, find someone
closer to your age.
Someone wise in wiles of women
who'd keep you guessing

instead of one who speaks her love,
who uses only soap
and water on her face,
expects her gift
to make up for no fancy wrapping.
Last night we found

empty spaces in one are filled
by the other; our strengths are multiplied.
Forgotten, this nonsense of who leads,
who responds. Movement produces
movement. One joyous cry
evokes another.

Flight of the Wild Goose

Someone I love
whittled a wild goose for me—
long wooden neck stretched out   eager
to catch each passing current of air
sensing this   avoiding that
with a sensuous twist of her lithe body.
Often she leaves her sister/brother geese,
veers about, wheels, circles
touching the others   only briefly
then off again on her own wild ideogram.

Yesterday we discovered all over again—
you and I are as unlike as two stars
or the whorls on our open palms.
Not to say you are better   or worse
because you follow a known path,
work tirelessly to get
things right, the way they're
meant to be,
come to decisions
with all deliberate care.
While I—well, I'm just a wild goose
flying away by myself
returning to touch   get my bearings
from you   before I double back
zoom out again.
Even a wild goose has to start from somewhere.

Unsnarling the Quarrel

We got ourselves into a snit.
How, nobody quite knew.

You thought I'd given you medical advice
which you took

and then began sneezing, working up to
almost an asthma emergency.

I thought you made a global
statement: "You tell me what to do."

I began defending myself
not realizing you weren't finished.

You said too many questions
weren't good either.

I said how can we understand
each other without *some* questions.

It took us nearly a week
to cool down enough to shovel out the slag,

begin all over, decide we do care
for each other, but, no, we're not "serious."

Your body gives you freedom to sleep tonight
after we spend our time

untangling, unraveling, unsnarling
what you said and what I said and what it all means.

I keep remembering long ago
when Dad and I readied our lines
for the next day, each evening repairing
the damage done by the day's casting.

Ugly, Crazy, Death Defying

"Hi, Ugly, how're you doin'?"
said one kid to another
lying in a hospital bed
his face half burned away.
Suddenly, our eyes connected.
I found I could look at him after all.

I remember my disbelief, as a social worker
in a psychiatric hospital,
when I first heard patients call each other "crazy,"
yet how, in some intangible way,
the air was cleaner, clearer,
as they labeled each others' behavior
the way it seemed to them.
Crazy, maybe, but real as a handful of dirt.

A friend shows me his Peak Flow Chart—
zigzag path of oxygen struggling to penetrate
pollen/stress clogged bronchial tubes.
One early-morning point dips
perilously lower than the rest.
My friend tells me, "Bad time, according to the doctors."

"A time when some people die," I find myself
saying—ugly, crazy words I hate
but know to be true.
I sense his shock at my words
and then   the meeting of our eyes.

Ne Répondez Pas Ainsi

Cleaning out my dresser drawer today,
I found a yellowed note, one I had
written to myself, years ago
when I was still struggling
with how to make a young marriage work.
I had written it in French,
a language my husband
did not know, on a scrap he would not notice.

*Ne répondez pas ainsi— répondez avec amour.**

After he died, I could not bear
to throw it away, kept it along
with other garnerings of fifty-two years.
Today, when I made myself a note
not to contradict my new man friend
nor give an impression I was—heaven forbid!—
telling him what to do, I came upon my
kindly old friend, good rule
for getting along with any human.

*Do not respond thus—respond with love.

48

When the Woman Is Older

You look at me and see your Mother—
anxious, controlling, a lady.
Ten years between is too long.

I look at you and wonder how
you happen to be still single.
You look at me and see your mother.

We seek waveringly to find
each other, to deny our differences.
Ten years between is too long.

I fall in love, or so I think.
You think of me, if at all, as a friend.
You look at me and see your Mother.

To your ears, my suggestions
begin to sound like demands made of a boy.
Ten years between is too long.

Your asthma worsens when I am around.
Between sneezes, you finally tell me off.
You look at me and see your Mother.
Ten years between is too long.

The River Meander

You and I are both Gemini—
no sooner do we
make up our minds one way
than another
seems infinitely more desirable.

Each of us has our own
pattern of handling
this two-sidedness.   You
like to mosey along   I gallop
ahead   then have to retrace

my steps. A little like
a switchback   long swoop ahead   then
sharp reversal
and another long swoop
flying in the direction I just came from.

Your moseying reminds me
of the River Meander   a tortuous
stream inland from the Aegean coast
so convoluted it takes
ten times

as long getting to the sea
as any normal river.
I have to keep reminding myself—
both the Meander   *and* switchback rivers
eventually reach their destination.

Cartoon Collage

Do you gauge your emotional temperature
by reading cartoons?
I do.

I like to wait
until my favorites
tell me something about the human condition
about me   about *us*
before deciding how *I* feel.
Then that shiver of recognition—

"There *we* are!"
Remember the cartoon I used to let you know
my feelings—"You'd think two people
as intelligent as we could find *some* way
to fall in love!"

Intimacy Avoidance

The trouble
with loving
a man who's scared
of being
intimate
with another human
is   I can't
just gather you up
in my arms and kiss
your mouth and ears and
the top of your dear curly head
and tell you I love you
and the world is really OK
after all (in spite
of what you were told
in body language all those years)
because if I did you'd run
right out the door
and never, never
come back.

Blowup to Blowup

We can be going along OK
nothing special   but still compatible
when one of us   usually you
each of us would say
shies off   paws the air   pounds
the ground with heavy hooves
whinnies pleadingly   allows wheedling to begin

and so we settle down   are mollified
start over   yearning to love   be loved
scared witless of giving it that name.
"You act as if we're engaged to be married,"
you say   just to make sure we're not.
"That takes mutual consent," I reassure you.

Half a Loaf

is better than no loaf at all
but how empty I felt with half, or less.

The aphorist who made up that aphorism
must have been a pauper   or restricted
to a strict 600 calorie diet.

For many years I enjoyed
a round and warmly fragrant loaf

redolent of herbs and good sweet butter.
Is that why I rebelled at what you
say is all the loaf you'll share?

Even while I yearned for more
I heaped sunflower seeds, molasses, bananas

into the loaf I shared with you.
I used to pretend your slender loaf was enough.
Sometimes I confused your gift with my

long-remembered abundance, persuaded myself
you surely loved me   when you were only giving

out of a need to be thought a good fellow
not because your hands found joy in making me a gift.

Now   three months since we shared bread
it's clear: half a loaf is all your child was given,
so half is what you have to share. I no longer expect more.

Mirrors

"You boggle my mind!"
your parting words.
I hope they'll fade in time
leaving only a soft glow.

To comfort myself
as on a screen I bring up
other mirrorings: my granddaughter
urging me to stay all night

my grandson's poem
to let me know
how he sees dandelions. Fathers
of those two making me feel important still.

When someone shows me how
I came across
in ways I never meant
or could not help

I cushion that blow
by remembering yellow, green
and blue images
burnished to a sheen.

Switching from Love to Friendship

It's always pleasant to know
where I'm going, so
I looked up "friendship"
in Webster's, found the first meaning:
"attached to another by affection or esteem."
There were others, but I liked that one best.

Now for where I'm coming *from*.
Love, as you might assume, was more
complicated. The first definition didn't fit
our situation, requiring kinship—maternal
ties the example. Exactly what I want
to avoid for the best of reasons: I am not your mother.

Then Webster's went wild.
God's love; holding one's opponent
scoreless at tennis; the object
of an attachment   all vied with the one
I meant when I said I loved you: attraction based
on sexual desire, affection, tenderness felt by lovers.

Note the plural. So that kind
of love is out for us. Friendship seems to be
our thing. A few days ago, that word paled
beside what I felt for you. Now it seems to be
just right, a simple garment both of us can wear
with ease. No anxiety. No stress. No commitment.

And if it lacks the zing and glow of love
it has what could be more lasting—mutual need.
If you agree, I'd be glad to get your call—friend.

Saturday Morning Dream Poems

1.

I wore a long gray pleated skirt.
I felt warm and protected by it.
Something tore or ripped or burned
a long gash in my skirt. At first
I thought I should throw it away
but found I could not do this.
Instead, I cut out the injured part
bound crimson silk to the underside.
I no longer wear my skirt
but often take it out and look at it.

*Saturday morning had been the time I anticipated our time
together. Now each week I'll take my dream temperature, learn
how I'm healing from our split.*

2.

Two lilies   one tall
shining white and green
the other clear yellow
slimmer   smaller
stand side by side in a marshy
spot   well shaded
bend with a gentle wind
sometimes touching. "Sure
you are content?" murmured the white lily,
"No longer yearn to be part of the river
plunging   gurgling   surging?
All day we hear its siren sound."
"Positive!" bobbed the yellow lily
bending close. "I finally learned—
lilies rarely live in rivers."

*This was the week we mended what felt like a severed
relationship, decided to settle for what each of us felt we could
freely give—friendship.*

3.

I am lying in bed, half-waking,
half-sleeping. I have a strong urge
to get up. Something splendid
is about to happen. I want to be ready.
But something keeps me in bed, somnolent,
unknowing. As long as I am unaware
maybe this new thing will not happen.
Maybe it is not splendid at all, the opposite.
I toss back and forth, forth and back
caught on the end of a skewer.

*This is the day before you come over. We will try out our new
relationship, see how it fits us, how much you will feel at ease,
how much I need to shrink expectations.*

Don't Look Back

except fleetingly
to see how far you've come
or to make sense out of a boilup
you had years ago   and never understood.

Distant colors
soften to violets and dim blues.

Shapes, even crazy jags
eventually wear themselves down.

So don't look too far forward
to see where you're going   and how soon
or try too hard to foresee
stumblebumps ahead.

Future colors
are vivid, often garish.

Shapes may be of people
you've not yet encountered.

Now seems to me the best time—
in simple primary colors,
shapes of simple people who return your caring.

Instant Identity Confirmation

As I slip my plastic card
into the slot at my bank's Express Window
the kindly woman/man inside
accepts it   takes my hand
leads me gently   firmly through a maze
of secret numbers   then offers me
two crisp twenties
and an approving pat.

I think I'll invent
a Lost Persons' Identity Bank
so   next time I'm not sure who I am
or if...
I can hand it my secret Identity Card
(which I will keep close to my skin)
and it will tell me
what name I'm known by,
whether anyone is waiting for me,
and nudge me in the right direction.

Poem

FOR MY SEVENTY-EIGHTH BIRTHDAY

My word processor
thought I ought to use
lower case—you know, small letters
for "seventy-eighth"—as if
it were only a small thing
to have lived so long.
You're *wrong*! I told my friend,
usually so helpful, kind, empathic.
It is an *honor* to be alive,
to be permitted—to still
like ripe red raspberries,
to plan to go for our first swim
of the season tomorrow
with my son and granddaughter,
to get a card made by my grandson, with maybe
a mite of help from his father, wishing
a Happy Birthday to Grandma Janet,
to have someone who came to measure my windows
for screens refer to me as "pretty sharp"
(even though the "for your age" hovered on his lips),
to get a note from someone important,
another from someone important to me.

To look ahead and see—as far as I *can* see—
which of course isn't all that far for any of us—
that life will be yellow and blue and green
as long as I'm around to enjoy bright, joyous colors,
smell fragrant waxy-pale gardenias, pick red
berries dripping with juice.

Core-Key

Until I moved
to my condominium apartment
I'd never heard of a core-key,
slim shiny-smooth opener of gates.

"Turn left, then right — if you're
on the inside," someone told me, "right,
then left when you're coming home again."
"And — take it easy!"

I'd fiddle and fiddle
using more and more force,
only rarely hitting the right combination,
willing it to consider my need to go in-or-out
above its duty as guardian of the gate.

Today, I nudged my core-key
gently, slowly left/right until
I felt it move beneath my hand, respond with alacrity
to my less demanding touch.

Feeling Myself into Animals and Birds

A good friend once
wrote I reminded her of a deer —
a young deer, a fawn.

How could she possibly
find a young deer in one so full
of years? I decided to try the part

ignore my slow legs, my not so youthful shape
soon found myself leaping and bounding
only infrequently stopping to sniff the air.

I like that feeling   bring it back
whenever life seems intent on tethering
me on all fours.

The other day   when flu prevented
even images of cavorting
another good friend sent me a postcard

photo of a gannet
rapt gaze
fixed on something in the sky

a mate perhaps   or God. She looked
transfixed by visions   inaccessible
to merely human eyes   clearly a spiritual being.

"I hope this Gannet is a Janet,"
she wrote, "and that you're both
looking up when this arrives."

Now   whenever I look down
or too inwardly, I feel myself into this creamy white bird
so confident of essential goodness   and look up.

Poem for a Distant Friend

Read this at your peril!
If you respond, it is sure
to be only the first among many.

I deluged my erstwhile suitor
kept hoping he'd catch fire
from my quickness to kindle

and constancy in steady glow. Alas,
(or maybe not) it did not happen.
So now I am adrift again   waiting to see

if the improbable can yet touch me
and someone known, unknown
or barely known. This at least

is something I can remedy. While you
are still three thousand miles
away, let me share a cross section:

My half-Siamese cat Blackie and I
share a two bedroom condominium apartment—
pines and liquid amber, curved walks, four pools.

Blackie bounces across my middle for a double-ear scratch
around seven, whittles this to six as winter wanes.
I turn on NPR for "Morning Edition," push fireplace button.

Breakfast! I cook oatmeal—two taps on my microwave
sometimes add a splash of Zoom, top this
with yogurt and a sliced banana. Coffee I eschew.

No husband to cook for, fat rice cakes
or English muffins are my staff.
Cranberry juice, grapefruit or a tangerine.

I rinse and stack my dishes, give my solitary bed
a daily fling. All other housework waits
until I've completed my poem or written letters.

Sometimes dusting waits a long time.
Piles of correspondence or ideas
accumulate without my noticing.

I love writing poems and plays
viewing what others have imagined, sharing
my work with others similarly inclined. Now

if this strikes you as a dull life
repels you with its austerity or lack
of firm control—well, this is what my life

is like these days. And if my letter fails
to make you flinch, take this as an invitation—
come visit me. Let's explore lunch, dinner   and beyond.

When the Temperature Hits 108

The hotter I get these days
of August, the more
I seem to think
about all those people
to whom I should have turned
the other cheek or thought twice
before I spoke
or not put my foot in my mouth—
clichés rise up and swat me angrily
upbraiding me for asking that famous poet
if he "really likes teaching"
furious that he appraised
my prosy poem as prosy.

Or the time I told a sister playwright
I thought her woman lead seemed
too exercised about feminism
considering her own good fortune.
Who am I to say—one play to my credit,
a beginner   rank as a baby skunk on the prowl.

Dozens of pointing fingers
await their turn—
begin to drum their way around
my overheated brain, make me wonder:
is it really the heat
or could this be yet one more
sign of my mortality?

I remember my sister, in the glare
of her darkened hospital room
suddenly asked if I thought
maybe *she* had something to do
with our mother's cool aloofness.
That was a December day, not August.
In the middle of her self-castigation,
my sister said bluntly, "I never knew dying
could take so long or be so ornery."

Connections

While waiting for the 8:06 bus
first day of autumn rain
roar and thud
of heavy machinery hauls me
out of my introspection.
Two yellow monsters
are working a runoff ditch
their wheels deep in fast flowing water.

One stays put, resting
while the other runs back and forth
between a jumble of shrubs, trees, and dirt.
With its prey, scoops
a huge mouthful
into its maw, then races
to deposit its prize in the waiting machine.

I only have time to wonder
who in the Department of Public Works
thought it would work better
to put off these fall cleanup jobs
until the rain forced action
when my bus appears   at 8:15. At my first class
I ask for another day to hand in my scenario.
Only this morning do I make
connections.

Faceless Enemies

Every spring morning
our condominium walk
is strewn with crushed bodies,
inner parts.
The snail marauders
who prowl our shrubbery
for tender leaves and buds leave
only skeletons.

Remembering my late sassy pink
geraniums, put out to welcome friends,
entice with vivid colors those
who might become friends,
my anger blooms each morning.

Today, I am tempted to smack down
a young snail
whose feeling stalks wave hopefully
in this early morning drizzle.

But I pass on by, leaving him
to more resolute stalkers.
I cannot bring myself to kill
what I abhor, even when faced
with nightly hordes of faceless enemies.

Striding through Rain

this Friday in March
as we surge out of waves
of buses in early morning,
pour by thousands
from cars and five wheelers
in near and far fingers
of parking in areas off
the flat palm of our campus,
all of us: black and white, brown
(bouquets in rainbow rain-gear)
take in rain-stirred new air
the pink blooming cherries
fragrant white blossoming apple
contouring their arms skyward—
and the brave way new grass tries
to make it, not squinch under each swishing step.

We remember what rain sounded like
last night as we spooned with our mate,
or, having none, remembered what spooning
felt like when we were among the fortunate.
And we listened to the PING ping ping
or the PING ping ping ping ping
or the unaccented thrum of the ping ping ping ping—
and all of us feel blessed by this gentle rain.

Just Past Black Shine

Do you hear the midsummer call of the wild blackberries?
A soft, seductive invitation.
A murmuring: full, ripe, ready.
Joyous song of a single juicy berry
as it slips down your parched throat.
Each day the call grows more insistent,
now a mosquito-buzz in your ear,
a plaintive fear of drying, unused, on the vine.
When I was younger, I picked only
blackberries shiny as new-washed faces;
even sweeter are those just past black shine
before the wrinkling and the shrinking.

Transparency

A loving woman
a sunlit flower   open
for all to enjoy

Janet Carncross Chandler

Janet Carncross Chandler holds an MFA in Writing from Goddard College (1988) and an MSW from the George Warren Brown School of Social Work, Washington University in St. Louis (1960). She was a social worker for thirty years prior to her retirement in 1971. She has since become a poet and in 1982 at the age of seventy-two published her first book of poetry, *The Colors of a Marriage*, which is in its fifth printing. She has self-published three other books: *Poems for Poets and Other Fragile Humans* (1983), *"How Are You?" They Ask New Widow* (1985), and *Significant Relationships* (1988). Her poetry has appeared in numerous poetry journals and she has authored three plays.

Ms. Chandler leads writers' groups at the Sacramento Poetry Center, the Robertson Adult Disabled Day Health Care Center, and the Renaissance Society. She is a member of the Unitarian Universalist Society of Sacramento and is an enthusiastic participant in Elderhostels.

Photo by Toni Sullivan

Lori Burkhalter-Lackey

Lori Burkhalter-Lackey was born and educated in Los Angeles, California, completing her photographic training at Otis/Parsons Art Institute. Her work has been exhibited in many California galleries and she recently completed several documentary photographic assignments in Paris.

In 1987 her work was featured prominently in a Papier-Mache Press anthology on women and aging. In 1988 her photographs accompanied the poetry of Sue Saniel Elkind in *Another Language*. She is currently working on a photographic documentary about homeless women and children.

Lori lives in Los Angeles with her husband David and their three cats.

Photo by David Lackey

Other Papier-Mache Press Books:

When I Am an Old Woman I Shall Wear Purple, an anthology of poetry, fiction, and photography exploring the issues of aging women, $10.00, 0-918949-02-5.

Another Language, poetic exploration of aging by septuagenarian Sue Saniel Elkind, photographs by Lori Burkhalter-Lackey, $8.00, 0-918949-05-X.

The Tie That Binds, Fathers & Daughters/Mothers & Sons, an anthology of poetry, fiction, and photographs about relationships between parents and children of the opposite sex, $10.00, 0-918949-04-1.

The Inland Sea, Poetry by Jenny Joseph, a selection from the poetry of the British author of "Warning—When I Am an Old Woman I Shall Wear Purple," $5.00, 0-918949-08-4.

Fragments I Saved from the Fire, short story collection by Mary Anne Ashley, illuminating the lives of the men and women who live on the fringes of society, $9.00, 0-918949-06-8.

If I Had a Hammer, Women's Work in Poetry and Fiction, an anthology of poems, fiction, and photographs exploring women's experience in the workplace, $11.00, 0-918949-09-2.